HIDDEN LIFE
of the DESERT

Second Edition

Thomas Wiewandt

2010
Mountain Press Publishing Company
Missoula, Montana

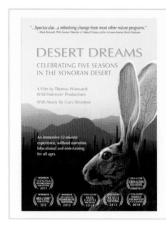

DESERT DREAMS
CELEBRATING FIVE SEASONS
IN THE SONORAN DESERT

"...Spectacular...a refreshing change from most other nature programs."
— Mark Dimmitt, PhD, former Director of Natural History at the Arizona-Sonora Desert Museum

A Film by Thomas Wiewandt
Wild Horizons Productions
With Music by Gary Stroutsos

An immersive 52-minute
experience, without narration.
Educational and entertaining
for all ages.

HIDDEN LIFE OF THE DESERT
is a companion book to the film
DESERT DREAMS, produced
by Thomas Wiewandt, and
available for viewing on public
television stations.

Library of Congress Cataloging-in-Publication Data

Wiewandt, Thomas A. (Thomas Alan)
  Hidden life of the desert / Thomas Wiewandt. — 2nd ed.
      p. cm.
  Includes bibliographical references and index.
  ISBN 978-0-87842-555-6 (alk. paper)
  1. Desert ecology—Southwest, New—Juvenile literature. 2. Desert ecology—Juvenile literature. I. Title.
QH104.5.S6W45 2010
577.540979—dc22

                                    2009048219

PRINTED IN HONG KONG

MP Mountain Press
PUBLISHING COMPANY
P.O. Box 2399 • Missoula, MT 59806 • 406-728-1900
800-234-5308 • info@mtnpress.com
www.mountain-press.com

For Victoria, Abby, Langdon,
and all who embrace sustainable living

ACKNOWLEDGMENTS

Bookmaking is a collaborative journey between authors, publishers, editors, and graphic designers. I wish to thank the team at Mountain Press Publishing for their patience and professionalism in the creation of this work, especially Jennifer Carey, who so competently carried the project to completion. Thanks are due too to Neil Soderstrom and Crown Books for Young Readers, who made the 40-page, 1990 edition of this book possible.

The last chapter of this book—"Facing the Future"— required a diverse assortment of pictures and graphics, many of which were generously provided by other photographers and organizations (see credits in the captions). Those who shared their expertise or opened doors for new photographic opportunities that helped to bring this synthesis to life include Professor Charles F. Hutchinson, Director of the University of Arizona's Office of Arid Lands Studies; Professor Milton Sommerfeld, algae specialist at Arizona State University; Mark Dimmitt, Director of Natural History at the Arizona-Sonora Desert Museum (ASDM); Christine Conte, Director of the ASDM's Center for Sonoran Desert Studies; National Park Service Fire Ecologist Perry Grissom; Leslie Johnston, University of Arizona's Creative Director for External Relations; staff at Eurofresh Farms (now owned by NatureSweet); Joshua Scott, CEO of 50-mile Farms; Thomas Beatty; desert dwellers Barbara Rogers and George & Diane Montgomery; neighbors with a state-of-the-art rainwater harvesting system, Jay Cole and Carol Townsend; Baja fisherman Tony Reyes; and folks at Tucson's Tohono-Chul Desert Park. Thank you all.

I'm also grateful to colleagues and friends who read the text of "Facing the Future" and offered valuable suggestions: Rick Brusca, Director of the ASDM; Sally Antrobus, freelance book editor; Daniel Beck, Professor of Biology at Central Washington University; Victoria Hamman (age 17); and Abby & Langdon Ernest-Beck (ages 12 and 9).

CONTENTS

FIVE
SEASONS

A typical Sonoran Desert landscape within Arizona's Saguaro National Park

Five seasons? From the holidays we celebrate to the foods we eat, daily reminders of *four* seasons come our way. As snow melts, leaf buds swell and Easter lilies bloom, sure signs of spring. In summer's warmth, fireflies flash and corn grows tall. With autumn's chill, pumpkins ripen, leaves drop, and birds fly south. And when frost creeps over the land, bears seek shelter for a long winter's nap. Weather patterns set seasonal rhythms of change.

But climates differ widely over Planet Earth, and seasonal changes differ too. Native people in parts of Australia speak of seven seasons. Each is based on the availability of traditional wild foods. In the tropics, where temperatures stay much the same year-around, month-to-month changes in rainfall can be dramatic. In such places, people live by a two-season calendar—a wet season and a dry season.

In this book, you will visit the northern part of the Sonoran Desert in the American Southwest. Creatures living here know five seasons of the year: spring, dry summer, wet summer, autumn, and winter. Early summer is hot and dry. The arrival of violent thunderstorms marks the beginning of wet summer. Gentler rains come in winter, giving the region two important rainy seasons.

Deserts typically receive less than 10 inches of rain in a year. Tucson, for example, may get as little as 5 inches or as much as 22 inches of rain in different years. A half-day's drive away near the California border, Arizonans sometimes see less than 1 inch of rain in a year. Farther south, Sonoran Desert landscapes change yet again with local conditions. Little rain falls along the Pacific coast of Mexico's Baja California. Instead of rain, plants get much of their moisture from coastal fog rolling in where the cold ocean meets the warm land.

All deserts have one thing in common—they are dry most of the time. Desert plants and animals never know exactly how much rain will fall or when it will come. And things dry up so quickly that a long-term shortage of moisture severely limits life in these places. So all living things must stay in tune with rain, ready for its coming and prepared for its going.

We think of deserts as hot as well as dry. The Sonoran Desert is "hot" for about nine months of the year, and Arizona is the sunniest state in the United States. In southern Arizona daytime temperatures reach the 70s by March and climb steadily to midsummer highs around 100 degrees Fahrenheit. Yet not all deserts are hot. Imagine needing a parka in the desert to keep from freezing. At the extreme, Arctic deserts far to the north are so cold, dry, and windy that few plants or animals can live there.

Three of North America's deserts have cold winters—the Mojave (mo-háh-vee), Chihuahuan (she-wáh-wun), and Great Basin Deserts. Freezing temperatures kill most cactuses and desert trees. Where winter temperatures often stay below freezing around the clock, you will see no cactus giants, just miles and miles of tough shrubs, grasses, and a few scattered trees.

Winters are milder in the Sonoran Desert. Here, tropical plants and animals that mainly occur farther south overlap with cold-hardy species of the north. And terrain in the region is surprisingly diverse—a mix of rugged mountains, shady canyons, open valley floors, and rolling sand dunes. Add to

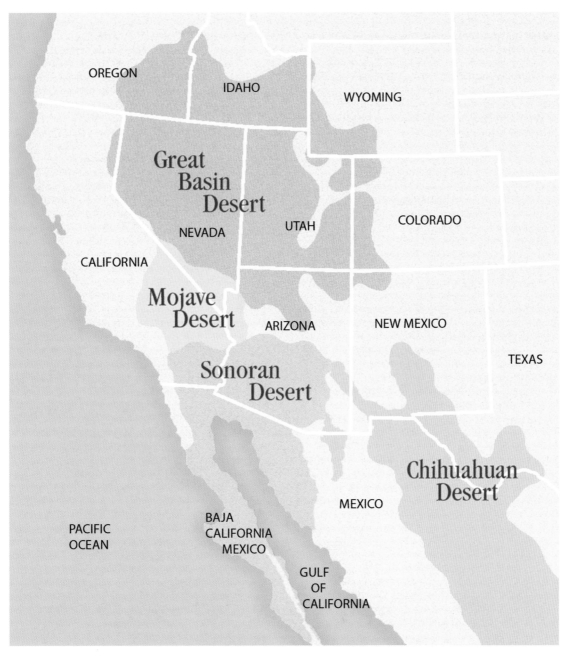

OREGON

IDAHO

WYOMING

Great
Basin
Desert

NEVADA

UTAH

COLORADO

CALIFORNIA

Mojave
Desert

ARIZONA

NEW MEXICO

TEXAS

Sonoran
Desert

Chihuahuan
Desert

MEXICO

PACIFIC
OCEAN

BAJA
CALIFORNIA
MEXICO

GULF
OF
CALIFORNIA

The four North American deserts

this its two rainy seasons, and the result is a wondrous desert that supports an exciting parade of plant and animal life. Considering all deserts, life in the Sonoran Desert is among the most richly diverse in the world!

As you will discover in the pages ahead, however, finding desert wildlife is not always easy. Just as desert plants have special adaptations to help them cope with heat, drought, and cold, animals have survival tricks too. Some have such clever ways to protect themselves from environmental extremes, you might not see them, even when they are right under your nose. Knowing *when* to look is as important as knowing *where* to look. Many animals are nocturnal (active at night) to avoid the daytime heat. The best times of day to find hidden life in the desert are early in the morning or in the evening, when it is cooler. The spring and summer seasons are the busiest. Use this book as your guide, and let spring begin.

Spring wildflowers: mostly Mexican gold poppy with owl's clover (purple) and desert lupine (blue) and a staghorn cholla cactus in the foreground

SPRING
Season of Color

Dune primrose (large white), sand verbena
(purple), and showy sunflower (yellow)

It has been a warm, wet winter in desert lands that stretch from southern Arizona into northern Mexico. The refreshing aroma of wet creosotebush fills the Sonoran Desert air. Gentle, soaking *female rains*, as some Native Americans call them, have softened rocky desert soils. Patches of green cover red earth. Wildflower watchers know this year will be special. Heavy autumn and early winter rainfall has set the stage. Seeds sprouted, winter temperatures stayed mild, and rains have kept coming.

Now in March, like magic, millions of sweet-smelling flowers appear. Such a sight comes only once every eight to ten years. Just weeks after blooming, these delicate plants will wither and vanish in the hot, dry air. Then their seeds must wait patiently for another wet year.

Mexican gold poppies growing alongside a cholla cactus skeleton

Spring wildflowers: mostly goldfields (yellow), with owl's clover (purple) and desert lupine (blue)

Warm spring days bring lizards above ground. Those that have stayed cool and asleep under rocks or within burrows all winter begin their search for food. For the desert iguana, eating creosotebush flowers is a joy of spring. But most lizards would rather hunt insects. Before starting to hunt each morning, lizards sunbathe to warm up. Many of these cold-blooded animals try to keep their daytime body temperature about the same as ours. An overheated collared lizard on a hot rock lifts his toes to keep from burning them. He will then dash for the shade to cool down.

Desert iguana eating creosotebush flowers

Collared lizard on a hot rock

At midday, as the temperature climbs and most lizards seek shade, zebra-tailed lizards remain active. These lean, long-legged lizards can tolerate high body temperatures. They are also among the fastest lizards in the West. Zebra-tails can run on two hind legs in explosive bursts of speed at 18 miles per hour. By comparison, the fastest human sprinter can run about 23 miles per hour.

Male zebra-tailed lizards try to scare away outsiders by standing tall and flattening the body from side to side to look as big and fierce as possible. Lizards use such body language to defend feeding and breeding territories and to attract mates. Many perform sets of "push-ups" or head-bobs to tell others of their kind to "Back off," or "Come closer."

A male zebra-tailed lizard displaying to another male nearby, threatening to attack if he doesn't back off

The Gila (HEE-la) monster is the only lizard in the United States with venom. It holds on with a vise-tight bite and chews venomous saliva into its prey. Few people are lucky enough to see one of these big, shy lizards in the wild. Gila monsters dig into rodent nests to steal the young, and they sometimes raid bird nests. Gambel's quail eggs are small enough to be swallowed whole in one big gulp!

Gila monster swallowing a quail egg

Gila monster

Western diamondback rattlesnake

Snakes also become active in spring. Rattlesnakes are well camouflaged, so watch your step. They strike quickly and inject venom through fangs, which are long, hollow, specialized teeth. When snakes (and most lizards) feed, they often break their teeth. New teeth grow to replace old ones, even in adults. So a rattlesnake that loses a fang at any age will get a shiny new one to take its place.

Rattlesnakes and Gila monsters flick their forked tongues to sniff the air for a scent of prey. The tongue carries chemical information to a special sense organ inside the mouth. Rattlesnakes often wait near rodent trails for a meal to come by. These "pit vipers" have heat-sensitive pits on the face in front of each eye, which they use to locate the position of their warm-blooded prey, even in the dark.

Lizards and snakes, beware! Even hunters may become the hunted. A roadrunner catches lizards for its chicks to eat. Insects, rodents, young birds, centipedes, and small snakes (even rattlesnakes!) are on the roadrunner's menu too.

Look closely and you'll see a horned lizard, a master at camouflage, hiding among the rocks.

Roadrunner feeding a lizard to its chicks

Most lizards run from danger, making them easy for roadrunners to spot. But horned lizards, with their short legs and wide bodies, aren't designed to be athletes. Naturally disguised to match their surroundings, they freeze in place to keep from being detected. A few lizards, such as chameleons, can quickly change colors to blend in. Horned lizards can't do this. They are born dressed in camouflage to match the rocks and soil where they live. Any born with the wrong colors are simply a well-advertised meal.

The sharp spines of cactus plants discourage animals from eating them. Here birds can find safe places to lay their eggs and rear their chicks. Like roadrunners, curve-billed thrashers build nests of sticks piled among the cactus spines. Like most birds, they abandon their nests when the chicks can fly. In contrast, the cactus wren weaves a grass-covered nest that is used as a home year-round.

Curve-billed thrasher chicks begging for food at a nest in a cholla cactus

Cactus wren nest in a prickly pear cactus

As spring temperatures rise, the blossoms of early wildflowers fade quickly in the heat. But now other flowers begin to appear. The Sonoran Desert becomes a wonderland of flowering trees, shrubs, and cactuses. Most can bloom every year because they store much food and water in their stems and roots. These tough plants are able to endure long periods of heat and dryness. Some have waxy or resinous coatings on their leaves and stems to reduce water loss. Those with fleshy stems—succulents—like cactuses and century plants, only open their stomata (pores for gas exchange) at night. This helps them to conserve moisture during the heat of day. And when times really get tough, they keep their stomata closed both day and night.

Flowers of a staghorn cholla cactus

Hedgehog cactus flower

Prickly pear cactus flowers

13

When the air is hot and dry, the leaves of many plants turn yellow and drop off. In times of drought, a leaf-fall protects desert plants from losing too much water through their leaves. The ocotillo (oh-koh-TEE-yoh), for example, is a woody wonder that blooms every spring, with or without leaves. Much of the year this strange plant looks like a spreading bunch of prickly dead sticks. But within three days after a rain, its branches can be covered with soft, green leaves. And as soon as the soil begins to dry, the leaves quickly turn yellow and fall off. This cycle repeats itself as often as rains come and go throughout the year.

Thirsty ocotillo plants preparing to drop their leaves to conserve moisture

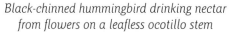

Black-chinned hummingbird drinking nectar from flowers on a leafless ocotillo stem

14

Flowering ocotillo stems bristling with leaves

Palo verde tree in bloom

Spring comes to a close while palo verde (PAL-oh VER-dee) trees bloom. They wear a veil of golden flowers. Unlike the ocotillo and most cactuses, this plant has very long roots that reach deep into the ground for water. The palo verde (a Spanish name which means "green stick") also has green bark. So even without help from its tiny leaves, the tree uses the sun's energy to make food through photosynthesis in its trunk and branches. This is helpful since it will lose its leaves both in the summer heat and in the cool of winter.

Mourning dove sitting on a leafless ocotillo branch

DRY SUMMER
Season of Scarcity

Flowering saguaro cactus

Dry summer begins in May, when palo verde blossoms fade and the giant saguaro (suh-WA-row) cactus blooms. Its white, waxy flowers open at night. Long-nosed bats swoop in to lap nectar from the blossoms. This sweet, energy-rich drink provides fuel and water for the bat. And, without knowing it, the bat helps the plant. Pollen grains that stick to the bat's fur hitch a ride from flower to flower, helping the plant to produce fruit and seeds. This same dependency between bats and flowers holds true for other giant cactuses and century plants.

Lesser long-nosed bat drinking nectar from century plant flowers

A saguaro cactus may grow taller than a four-story building (50 feet). These giant cactus trees become living apartment houses. Gila woodpeckers peck out nest cavities in the fat stems. Quickly the plant seals the wound with a corky covering that protects against water loss and infection. Each family of woodpeckers makes at least one new nest hole every year. When they move out, other birds, such as elf owls, move in. The elf owl stands only 5 inches high—it is the smallest owl in the world. These tiny owls hunt for insects and scorpions at night.

Gila woodpecker at its nest hole in a saguaro cactus

Elf owl with its chick inside an artificial saguaro at the Arizona–Sonora Desert Museum

Bark scorpion with day-old babies on her back

Scorpions also hunt their favorite foods at night. They sting insects to paralyze them, which keeps their meal from running away. Scorpions do not lay eggs. Baby scorpions are born and at birth crawl onto their mother's back. She protects her young but does not feed them. After a week, these tiny scorpions leave their mother and start to hunt insects for themselves.

19

Water supplies become scarce in dry summer. Animals may find precious pools of water in shady canyon bottoms or close to human dwellings. Desert cottontails, mule deer, and Gambel's quail drink daily if water is near. Quail eggs begin to hatch in early summer. Within an hour after hatching, the chicks are alert, feathered, and ready to run.

Male (left) and female (right) Gambel's quail

Gambel's quail chicks

Desert cottontail drinking

Round-tailed ground squirrels dig burrows that stay cool even when soil at the surface becomes painfully hot. Cool burrows offer a comfortable place to hide from the midday sun. These mammals also have the unusual ability to raise and lower their body temperature as air temperatures rise and fall—something we can't do. This saves them energy.

Ground squirrels are an important part of the desert food web. Coyotes, badgers, predatory birds, and snakes love to snack on them. Snakes can slide into squirrel burrows to search for helpless young, but round-tailed ground squirrels do have a clever defense. When a snake enters one of their burrows, a group of squirrels will immediately begin filling the entrance hole with dirt. If they can plug the snake's only exit to the surface, the intruder will be trapped underground, perhaps buried alive!

Antelope jackrabbit

Jackrabbits don't use underground burrows to escape the midday heat. They rest in the shade under bushes. Their huge, thin ears help them keep cool. On clear, hot summer days, jackrabbits can radiate heat from their ears—blood flowing through them loses heat before it returns to the body.

Antelope jackrabbit keeping cool in the shade

"Howling" grasshopper mouse

The fierce little grasshopper mouse howls to communicate with others of its kind, much like a coyote. But its howl is a high-pitched scream—nearly beyond the range of human hearing. Also like the coyote (see page 54), the grasshopper mouse is a hunter. Although most mice eat plants, this one prefers insects, scorpions, and lizards.

Grasshopper mouse attacking a cactus longhorn beetle

Another rodent, the kangaroo rat, never needs to drink. From seeds and other dry foods it eats, this large jumping mouse makes water within its body and can use it again and again. Like kangaroos, these mice use their hind legs for hopping and their long tails for balance.

Kangaroo rat

Conenose bug, or "kissing bug," sucking blood from a packrat

Rodent nests are breeding grounds for conenose bugs. Like mosquitoes, these insects get food and water by sucking blood from larger animals. Their bites can hardly be felt. The bug's sharp beak injects saliva that contains chemicals to numb the nerves and keep the victim's blood flowing. Conenose bugs bite people too, and they are commonly called "kissing bugs." The bugs earned this name by giving people an unfriendly "kiss" near the mouth as they sleep. The swelling caused by the bite is often large and very itchy.

White-winged doves feeding on saguaro cactus fruit

In June, living things in the Sonoran Desert must face their greatest challenges from the extreme heat and drought of dry summer. You'll see stressed birds and mammals panting in the shade. To conserve water and energy, some animals go underground. Others, such as rattlesnakes, are now active only at night, a cooler time of day when many rodents are running about. Just when water and green leaves are most scarce in the desert, one saving grace is unfolding: cactus fruit.

As saguaro fruits ripen, they swell, split, and curl open into blazing red stars. From a distance you might think they are flowers. Each fruit's tough outer shell bears a sweet surprise inside: a juicy mass of red pulp the size of a chicken egg, packed with shiny black seeds. Any creature that can fly will be first to be served—birds, bats, moths, and more. Countless other animals, coyotes included, eagerly await fruits that fall to the ground. Large saguaro arms offer dozens of fruit, so there is plenty to go around. This dry-season banquet is truly a lifesaving feast for many desert animals.

Saguaro cactus fruit

Juanita Ahil, a member of the Tohono O'odham tribe, using a pole made from the skeleton of a saguaro cactus to harvest saguaro fruit

Native Americans who have traditionally depended upon wild foods in the Sonoran Desert also look forward to cactus fruit. The Tohono O'odham, or Desert People, harvest saguaro fruit using a pole made from the woody skeleton of a dead saguaro (see photo on page 51). They boil and strain the seedy fruit pulp to make syrup, jam, seed meal, and wine. The Desert People honor the saguaro and drink ceremonial wine to ask for rain. And every year the rains do come.

Summer monsoon storm

WET SUMMER
Season of Surprises

Just when time seems to be standing still in the summer heat, wind changes direction and begins to blow from the coast of Mexico. These monsoon winds bring moist air, and clouds start to form. As thunderstorms build in late afternoon, the air becomes charged with electricity. Spectacular lightning shows begin.

Saguaros with an electrical storm in the distance

Dramatic thunderhead lit by lightning at twilight

Wet summer sunset

The wet season of summer arrives in late June or early July with high winds and driving rains. The rain may be so heavy that it rushes down hillsides before it can soak into the ground. *Arroyos* (dry streambeds) fill quickly. Each storm is brief—these flash floods normally last less than an hour. And when sunshine greets the rain, rainbows appear.

Flash flood in an arroyo

Desert downpour

Wet-summer afternoon rainbow

For many desert creatures, summer's first flooding rain begins a new year. The rumble of thunder and the pounding of raindrops on the desert floor tell spadefoot toads that it is time to wake up. Nature's alarm clock has awakened them from ten months of sleep underground.

Spadefoot toad awakened by heavy summer rain

Eye of a spadefoot toad

Male spadefoot toad calling for females

Male spadefoot toads hop to nearby rain puddles and call, "Eeeoow, eeeoow, eeeoow." This loud song attracts females. When a female comes close, the male grabs her tightly around the waist. As the two then swim together, she lays eggs and he releases a nearly invisible cloud of sperm into the water, a mating ritual called *spawning*. His sperm fertilize the eggs, starting their growth.

Spadefoot toads spawning

Spadefoot toad burying itself

Freshly laid spadefoot egg masses

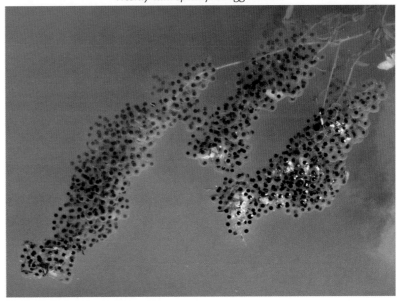

This burst of activity continues all night. At sunrise, each toad leaves the water and hops off alone. Using their rear feet, spadefoots dig new holes, where they can safely sit and wait for another very wet night. Then they will hunt for insects. To make it through a year of sleep underground, spadefoots need only one big meal.

Once spadefoot toad eggs are fertilized, the young must develop from egg to tadpole to tiny toad before the puddle dries up. A tadpole must grow lungs and legs before it can crawl onto dry land. Only then is it ready for life as a toad. Desert spadefoots can finish the race from egg to fully formed froglet in just ten days.

Spadefoot eggs

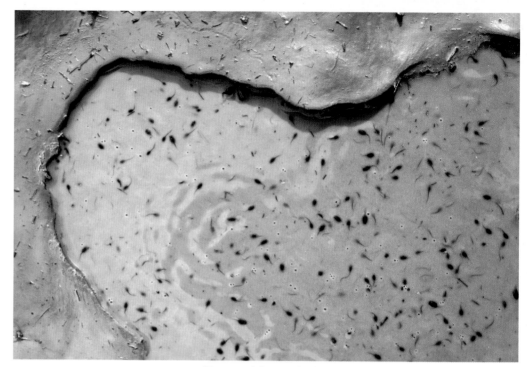

Tiny spadefoot tadpoles

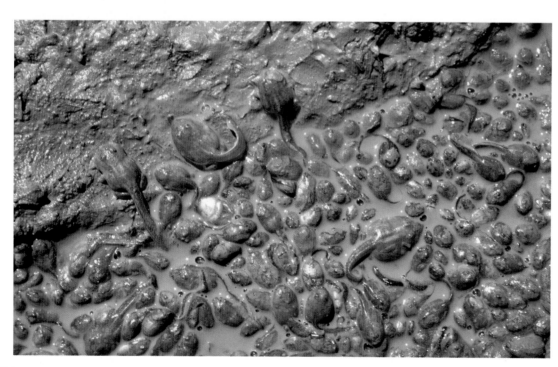

Spadefoot tadpoles race to become toads before their pond dries up—those without legs won't finish this race.

Spadefoot tadpoles have the unusual ability to "shape-shift." Eating different foods can dramatically change what they will look like as they grow. Young tadpoles that feed mostly on algae and decaying matter become small-headed tads. And those that eat fairy shrimp become big-headed morphs. The more animal matter a tadpole eats, the faster it will grow. These big-headed carnivores even eat their smaller brothers and sisters!

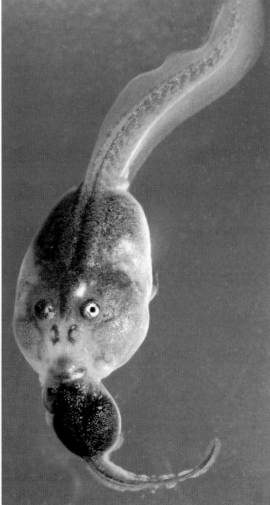

One spadefoot tadpole eating another

Spadefoot tadpoles with a fairy shrimp

Desert millipede

Defensive coil of a desert millipede

There are giants in the desert, with eight legs or more: 4-inch spiders, 6-inch millipedes, and 9-inch centipedes. All insects have six legs and three main body parts—head, thorax, and abdomen. All spiders have eight legs with two body segments—a head fused to its thorax and an abdomen. And both millipedes and centipedes grow long, slender bodies with lots of segments and more legs than you would want to count. Rain brings many of these creatures above ground in search of food, water, and mates.

After summer storms, rainworms—desert millipedes—are sometimes seen crossing roads by the thousands. They eat moist leaf litter but will also nibble on the bark of creosotebush, ocotillo, and other desert shrubs. Rainworms begin life with only six legs and can add another two hundred to three hundred as they grow. Their legs are short, so millipedes cannot scurry away from hungry animals. Instead, if attacked, they curl into a tight coil and release a nasty-tasting fluid through openings along the body.

Although related to millipedes, centipedes have longer legs and only one pair of legs per body segment. Millipedes have two pair—that's four legs per segment. Centipedes can move quickly and actively hunt at night. The giant desert centipede eats insects but will sometimes capture small reptiles and rodents. In turn, many large reptiles, mammals, and birds will tackle these tasty slithering giants. To avoid a centipede's painful bite, smart predators should attack the head end first. But which end is which? This confusing choice may give the centipede a chance to escape.

A Word of Warning: *Do not handle centipedes with your bare hands—their bite is one you will never forget! Left alone, they run away from people. Human deaths from centipede bites are rare—worldwide, only three have been reported in the last one hundred years. Even honeybee stings are much more dangerous.*

Giant desert centipede

Huge hairy spiders called tarantulas may seem scary, but they are gentle creatures that rarely bite people. On damp summer nights, you might find a large male wandering about, searching for a mate. These animals are slow-growing and take eight to ten years to mature—a long time for a spider. Somewhat fatter than males, female tarantulas usually stay hidden in underground burrows. Here they wait patiently for visitors of many kinds. Insects looking for a dark, cool hideaway get an unpleasant greeting at Ms. Tarantula's door! Spiders help us by eating many insect pests . . . fewer kissing bugs would be nice.

Male desert blond tarantula

Giant red velvet mites

When flooding rains bring swarms of winged termites above ground, mighty mites among spiders might appear too. Giant red velvet mites are about the size of a pea, and they only eat termites. Up close, these mites resemble tiny tanks dressed in fuzzy red suits that fit a little too loose. Their red color warns predators that they taste bad. Seeing bright red dots on the desert floor always comes as a surprise. A curious helicopter pilot once spotted a dense patch of thousands from the air. Velvet mites must fatten up on termites, mate, and lay eggs in just a few days, before retreating underground for another year, or two, or more . . . no one knows for sure.

In wet summer, when the fruit of prickly pear cactuses ripen, feasting begins. If you meet a desert tortoise with her face stained red or purple, she has surely been enjoying cactus fruit. Tortoises are turtles that live on dry land. Like all turtles, tortoises never grow teeth. Instead, they have a sharp beak that cuts food. Birds peck holes in cactus fruit to reach the sweet, juicy pulp inside. Then insects, such as the golden paper wasp, can eat the leftovers.

Desert tortoise eating prickly pear cactus fruit

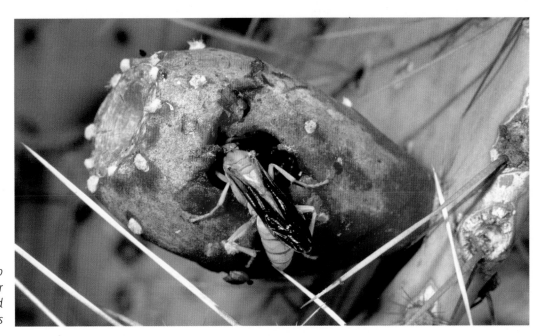

A golden paper wasp enjoying a prickly pear cactus fruit pecked open by birds

39

Wet season's bounty of seeds, insects, flowers, and fruit has kept the cactus mouse happy. Like all desert survivors, this dainty little creature must cope with difficult times too. And it can. As you might expect, the cactus mouse is active at night and sleeps during the day. But it can change its sleeping habits. When food and water are scarce, the cactus mouse can lower its body temperature and burn less energy. It can also sleep through long hot dry spells, falling in and out of deep sleep, called *estivation*. With the arrival of autumn—the Sonoran Desert's second dry season—this little mouse is ready for whatever may come.

For the cactus mouse, moving just one prickly pear fruit is a struggle!

The Sonoran Desert's second dry season

AUTUMN
Season of Change

A mature male lubber grasshopper on a leafless ocotillo stem

As summer leaves fade away and grasses go to seed, the Sonoran Desert's second dry season begins. Clouds vanish in September as wet summer gives way to autumn, a time of sunny days and chilly nights. As the soil dries, grasses turn to soft shades of gold, rust, and umber. Ocotillos quickly drop their leaves once again. But cactuses and many trees stay green. Changes in the landscape can be slow, and easy for people to miss. Insects, on the other hand, don't miss a beat. Autumn nights come alive with the music of cricket songs. And desert days are jumping with grasshoppers. You'll see splashes of color from butterflies too.

Horse lubber grasshoppers are big—among the biggest in the American West—and beautiful. Surprised by their size, some people joke that lubbers are as big as Chihuahuas. Not quite! But 3-inch lubbers are common. Each evening they climb to the tops of bushes to roost for the night. Here they are safer from predators and can warm up quickly in the morning sun. Actually, grasshopper mice, praying mantis insects, and centipedes are among the few creatures known to dine on them. They have a very foul flavor—bad enough to discourage most predators.

You are more likely to see horse lubbers walking than flying. Only mature males have wings long enough for flight. But they use them less for flying than for scratching out a tune to attract females. Like most other grasshoppers, females bury their egg cases in soil. Eggs hatch the following year. The tiny grasshopper hatchlings feed and grow during the summer months, reaching adult size in autumn.

Painted ladies, monarchs, queens, and fritillaries are just a few of the butterflies in the Sonoran Desert at this time of year. They gather on damp soil to sip water and minerals, and on flowers to sip sweet nectar, their fuel for flying. One amazing flier—the monarch—can travel south from Arizona to faraway mountains near Mexico City, where they spend the winter. The following spring they return to the United States, a round-trip journey of more than 2,500 miles. That's like flying from New York to Los Angeles without guidance from a compass or protection in an airplane!

Monarch butterfly tagged by biologists in Phoenix

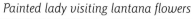

Painted lady visiting lantana flowers

Gulf fritillary on desert marigold

43

Fruits of the fishhook barrel cactus ripen to lemon yellow in autumn, a tempting snack for Harris' antelope squirrels. With the agility of an acrobat, a squirrel can scamper over the sharp, curved spines to reach the plant's golden crown. But claiming the prize is no easy task. The squirrel must grab the big fruit in its teeth and work it loose while balancing in a bed of daggers—quite the feat for such a fragile-looking animal! Curve-billed thrashers take the easy way: they leave the fruit where it is and poke holes in its thick flesh to get the nutritious pulp and seeds inside.

Harris' antelope squirrel gathering cactus fruit

Curve-billed thrasher eating cactus fruit

44

The collared peccary (PECK-uh-ree) is one of the few animals that can enjoy both cactus fruit and cactus stems—spines and all! Peccaries, also called *javelinas* (have-uh-LEE-nuz), are New World mammals—they range from North America to South America. They are not pigs. True pigs are native only to the Old World—Europe, Asia, and Africa. But they *are* distant cousins. Pigs and peccaries are more closely related to each other than to any other living mammals. Peccaries travel in small family groups in the Sonoran Desert. Babies are born throughout the year. In cool autumn weather peccaries wander and feed all day long, snacking on prickly pear cactus, grasses, roots, shrubs, insects, and even the remains of dead animals.

A family of collared peccaries

A collared peccary pausing to yawn while munching on a prickly pear pad

Collared peccaries, also called javelinas

Desert broom releasing its seeds in the wind

In November, as autumn nights grow colder, seeds of the desert broom float away on the wind. And where mountain streams flow to the desert floor, you can find water-loving broadleaf trees such as cottonwood, sycamore, and ash. At this time of year, their leaves turn yellow and orange and then fall off, just as in northern forests.

Autumn color in a desert canyon

Leafy plants that grow along streams attract animals you won't see in the open desert. White-tailed deer come down from the mountains. These deer are so wary that Native Americans have named them the "gray ghost" because they can quickly vanish into the thin brush. When alarmed, white-tails often stamp their feet, snort, whistle, and wave their raised tails. These signals tell predators they have been spotted and tell other deer that danger is near. When fleeing, they bound away with tail raised like a white flag, perhaps showing friends and family the way to safety.

White-tailed deer

Moonrise on a clear autumn night

In autumn, desert plants and animals prepare for winter. Elf owls fly south to warmer places in Mexico. There they will be able to find insects to eat in the cold months ahead. Reptiles slow down, and tortoises dig deep into the ground. Round-tailed ground squirrels spend more time in their burrows, storing seeds and preparing for winter sleep. Tiny seeds from spring's wildflower bloom lie dormant in the soil. Before winter cold sets in, they need at least one heavy rain to trigger their growth. Then, for the seedlings to survive, a mild winter must come.

After a desert snowstorm

WINTER
Season of Rest

You can be certain that winter has begun when nighttime temperatures dip below freezing. December storms move into the desert from the north, bringing cold air and soft gray clouds that blanket the sky. Gentle winter rains may last a day or two, with no thunder or lightning. Rain sometimes turns to snow, but it melts fast. After sunrise, the temperature can climb 30 degrees Fahrenheit in just a few hours.

Without snow, desert landscapes in December look much the same as in November, but usually fresher. Winter is, after all, the second wet season here. Most of the trees still have leaves, and cactuses can once again fatten up with rainwater. By January, cold nights force most trees to drop their leaves.

Snow is rare in this desert. It may be a winter treat for people but not for cactuses. Their juices protect them only against light freezes. In northern parts of the Sonoran Desert, many cactuses suffer from frostbite. The saguaro cactus may live for two hundred years, but a day or two of freezing cold can kill them. Cold is the number one killer of saguaros in Arizona.

A rare Sonoran Desert snowstorm

A large saguaro cactus weighs about 6 tons (12,000 pounds), which is more than a big elephant weighs. This great weight is supported by a woody internal skeleton. A freeze-damaged saguaro might look normal for several years, but as it begins to weaken, its heavy arms twist and droop. Bacteria, fungi, and insects invade the dying saguaro's flesh. Its trunk darkens and drips smelly brown ooze. Soft parts rot and collapse. All that remains are the saguaro's woody rib cage, pieces of leathery skin, and calluses that resist rapid decay.

Cactus skeletons come in many shapes and textures. The saguaro skeleton looks like a circle of sticks—called ribs—fused together in places. The woody remains of prickly pear pads are flat and fibrous, similar to rough, loosely woven cloth. Cholla skeletons are strong hollow cylinders pierced by a network of holes (see the photo on page 6). Honeybees, scorpions, birds, and many other creatures make their homes in cactus skeletons. And some live there year-round.

Saguaro cactus skeleton

Honeybee hive in a saguaro cactus skeleton

Great horned owl

Lizards, snakes, toads, and rainworms stay underground in winter. Most are in deep sleep, barely living but healthy. Some warm-blooded animals are also asleep. To save energy in winter, round-tailed ground squirrels turn down their body's furnace. They slow their heart rate, use less oxygen, and lower their body temperature—they hibernate. But, unlike reptiles and amphibians, they can't sleep straight through the winter. Every week or two, ground squirrels must wake up to refuel their bodies. They snack on food they have stored in their burrows. Then they curl up for another long snooze.

Harris' hawk

Other creatures remain active through much of the winter. Some, like bobcats, hawks, and great horned owls, are well adapted to the cold. Their fur or feathers keep their bodies warm. With many of their favorite foods still scampering about, Harris' hawks and great horned owls can begin nesting in January or February. Kangaroo rats and antelope squirrels are still gathering seeds, and jackrabbits are still outrunning coyotes.

Bobcat

Coyotes and foxes are well prepared for cold weather too—their fur thickens in winter to keep them warm. The kit fox is the smallest fox in North America. It weighs less than the average house cat. Like other foxes and coyotes, it digs an underground den, hunts small animals, and eats wild fruits. For a coyote, a kit fox or a house cat would be a prize worth catching!

Kit fox with an itch

A coyote in its winter coat

54

The largest animals in North American deserts are mule deer and bighorn sheep. Long ago, both species lived only in colder places far to the north. Over time, these cold-hardy animals spread south and adapted to desert conditions. Still, they often need more water than they can get from the plants they eat. In dry weather, they prefer to drink every day or two if surface water is available. They can sniff out small pools of water hidden in the desert. But when plants are wet with winter dew and full of moisture, these large mammals can go weeks without extra water.

When water gets really scarce, mule deer and bighorn sheep have special tricks for survival. Mule deer can smell water below the surface in dry streambeds, and they can dig for it by scraping sand away with their large hooves. A bighorn sheep can kick the top off a barrel cactus or butt a saguaro with its horns to reach the plant's juicy flesh inside.

Mule deer have big ears, like mules. Excellent hearing and sharp eyesight allow them to detect danger far away. They are quick, agile runners. In a calm and calculating manner they can outmaneuver predators in rough landscapes, and even climb cliffs. Males, called bucks, grow antlers, which fall off after the mating season and grow back the next year. Females, called does (singular doe, rhymes with TOE), have no antlers. In the Sonoran Desert, mule deer bucks court does and breed in winter. But most of the year, bucks prefer to be alone.

Mule deer doe

Mule deer buck

55

Bighorn sheep ram

Bighorn sheep live in rugged, rocky desert terrain with steep cliffs, where they can easily find shade and escape from coyotes and cougars (also called mountain lions). Rams (male bighorns) have large, curved horns, which grow longer and thicker every year and never fall off. In August and September, males need heavy horns to compete with each other for females in fierce head-to-head butting matches. You can hear the loud cracking of colliding horns from up to a mile away. Female sheep are called ewes (singular ewe, pronounced YOU). Ewes don't fight, and they have much shorter, thinner horns. Lambs are born all year round, but most births occur in late winter.

*Bighorn sheep
ewe with lamb*

In February, quail chatter as they peck at tender grasses and spring wildflowers that will soon burst into bloom. Hummingbirds and elf owls that overwintered in Mexico are migrating north. Cactus wrens are preparing to breed, as they freshen their nests by lining them with feathers. And on warm sunny days, you might spot a lizard poking its head out of hiding. Excitement is building. Come March, winter's peace will be broken by a fiesta of new life, starting the cycle of seasons once again.

Mountain lion (cougar)

FACING
THE
FUTURE

Spring in Organ Pipe Cactus National Monument, Arizona

As we have seen, the Sonoran Desert is filled with a great diversity of life and beauty. Wild plants and animals have fine-tuned their ways for successful living in this demanding environment. Those that don't adapt, perish. Harsh temperatures and scarce, unpredictable rainfall rule here. Over thousands of years, desert regions can grow or shrink under natural cycles of climate change. When the climate gradually becomes hotter and drier, deserts slowly expand. And their diverse communities of living things spread into neighboring areas. But how do people fit into this story? Have we come to the desert as a friend or foe? What does the future hold for our fellow creatures, and for us?

About one-third of the land on Earth is desert or nearly desert. And about three of every twenty people in the world now live in these arid and semiarid regions. For many centuries, people found ways to prosper in the desert without destroying it. They harvested native plants and animals for food. They collected and diverted rainwater. And they planted fast-growing crops that could tolerate drought. Native tepary beans, for example, can survive a month or more with no rainfall or irrigation. With some irrigation, these plants can run the race from seed to a mature crop in as little as two months.

Tepary bean plant (top)
Tepary beans and their seed pods (bottom)

Explosive population growth in the arid Southwest as seen in St. George, Utah

60

Degraded ranchland in the Sonoran Desert of Mexico
—Photo © Mark Dimmitt

Today natural deserts are vanishing as people overtax arid lands. Human activities have created new deserts of the worst kind—barren, nearly lifeless expanses of dry land. This happens when native plants have been stripped away for livestock, for firewood, or for other uses. Plants add moisture to the air, trap rainwater, and keep fertile soil from blowing away. With fewer plants, the air becomes drier, and less rain will fall. As the land becomes drier, erosion increases. Such man-made deserts spread quickly—by as much as 30 miles a year in some places. Drylands degraded through bad land-use practices lose their capacity to support native plants, wildlife, or people.

Farming is a major cause of land degradation. Water can be found deep underground in some desert areas, and it can be pumped to the surface for irrigation. But all groundwater contains dissolved mineral salts. Within a few years, irrigating with groundwater leaves a build-up of salts in the soil, and crops can no longer grow. This process is called *salinization*. Fields are often abandoned and left in a wasted state. Degraded farmland in rural Mexico, for example, is now forcing more than half a million people each year to search for new jobs in cities. Salt can be removed from water, but desalinization is a costly process that also makes concentrated, salty wastewater. Dumping this brine into a river kills freshwater plants and animals. And piping it into the ocean can kill marine life.

WANTED

Buffelgrass

DEAD AND GONE

Ranching has had a big impact on deserts of the American West. Cattle pollute freshwater supplies, trample young plants, and eat shrubs needed for wildlife habitat. Making matters worse, ranchers have planted exotic grasses to fatten their cattle. African buffelgrass has become a serious enemy. This weedy grass spreads quickly and is now invading all of our southwestern deserts. It produces fluffy seeds, lots of them, carried by wind far into the desert and even up mountainsides. Its seeds are also prickly enough to "hitch a ride" on animals. Buffelgrass is hardy and out-competes native plants for soil nutrients and water.

Buffelgrass also fuels intense fires. Without invasive grasses, the Sonoran Desert is nearly fireproof. Native desert plants don't grow close enough to their neighbors for fire to jump easily from one plant to another. Under natural conditions, desert fires stay small and burn out quickly. But a thick carpet of buffelgrass fuels

Invasion of buffelgrass in natural desert with organ pipe, saguaro, and cholla cactuses in northern Sonora, Mexico —Photo © Mark Dimmitt

hot wildfires that can reach 1,600 degrees Fahrenheit! Hot fires kill cactuses, palo verde trees, desert tortoises, and everything else caught in the blaze. Yet burned buffelgrass doesn't die. It regrows quickly, choking out native plants that try to repopulate scorched areas.

African buffelgrass is here to stay, but some residents of Arizona are fighting back. Volunteers in Tucson and Phoenix are pulling buffelgrass to stop its spread into new areas, especially desert parklands. They call themselves the Sonoran Desert Weedwackers. Their small but locally effective efforts have helped to prevent costly fires and to focus attention on the problem. The Weedwackers have joined other nonprofit and government organizations to form a Buffelgrass Working Group, now part of the Southern Arizona Buffelgrass Coordination Center.

Desert tortoise killed in a wildfire —Photo © Lesley DeFalco

Blazing desert wildfire fueled by exotic grasses —Photo © Tom Story

Barrel cactus in a charred desert landscape —Photo © Jan Emming

Desert sand dunes closed to ORV traffic (above) *and across the road* (below), *an area left open to ORVs, photographed on the same day*

The Sonoran Desert is fragile in other ways that we are just beginning to realize. The noisy off-road vehicles (ORVs) some people drive through the desert for fun have some unexpected effects. Spadefoot toads confuse sound vibrations from roaring ORV engines with natural signals coming from thunder and rain. Toads waking up in the dry season expect to find water and food when there's none to be found. Imagine the consequences. ORVs quickly degrade desert plant communities too. Sand dunes without ORV traffic support ten times more plant species than those heavily used by ORVs.

Scientists are also beginning to understand the importance of living "soil crusts" that carpet much of the desert floor. Biological soil crusts are complex communities of bacteria, algae, mosses, and lichens. With a trained eye, you can spot these living crusts on the surface of desert soils, but you would need a microscope to see most of the actual organisms clearly. They glue soil particles together, forming a living skin only a few millimeters thick. Like rooted plants, crusts help to keep soil from blowing or washing away. This thin fabric of organisms also holds moisture and adds nourishment to the soil in the form of nitrogen and carbon. Land clearing, ORVs, and trampling by cattle break up this fragile surface layer. Recovery is exceedingly slow and depends on soil type, climate, and the amount of damage—estimates of recovery times range from 2 to more than 3,800 years.

Scanning electron micrograph of sticky blue-green algae (hand-colored) among sand grains in living soil crust
—Image courtesy of Jayne Belnap

Wasteful watering of farmland near Yuma, Arizona
—Photo courtesy of the U.S. Bureau of Reclamation

Explosive human population growth, water shortages, and invasive species such as buffelgrass are the biggest challenges facing the American Southwest. Utah, Arizona, and Nevada, are among America's fastest growing states. In 2014, 61 percent of Arizona's 6.7 million people lived in Maricopa County—the state's capital city of Phoenix and its suburbs. Unfortunately, laws that govern the use of land and water have not kept up with changing times. In most of Arizona, for example, it is legal for developers to sell "dry lots" and homes without a dependable water supply. And under Arizona law, landowners who attempt to protect their land in a natural state pay 60 percent higher taxes than those who build houses on it. Water for desert agriculture is so cheap that farmers continue to plant inappropriate, moisture-loving crops, such as lettuce, cotton, alfalfa, and pecans. If all of the water needed in Arizona each year could fit into a one-quart bottle, only one cup of water would be left for everyone else after farmers took their share. And farmers make up less than 0.5 percent of Arizona's labor force.

About 43 percent of Arizona's water comes from wells. In the desert Southwest, people have been pumping out groundwater faster than Mother Nature can replace it. This has caused the earth to sink in some places. Sinking ground can crack sidewalks, roads, and the walls of your home. More than 1,700 sinks have been found in the Santa Cruz floodplain in southeastern Arizona. Just one hundred years ago, early pioneers fished from boats on the Santa Cruz River. Huge cottonwood, willow, and walnut trees once lined its banks. Today, the Santa Cruz is no longer a river. It has become a naked "arroyo" along most of its length. Leafy shade trees are gone and cannot be replanted. Their roots can no longer reach water.

The demand for water keeps growing in the Southwest. To help meet its needs, Arizona built a controversial 336-mile canal to carry water across the state. Completed in 1992, the Central Arizona Project (CAP) aqueduct brings in water from the Colorado River all the way to Tucson. Unfortunately, this great river—the lifeblood of the Southwest—is no longer great. Snowmelt in the Rocky Mountains feeds the Colorado River; but with the rise of global warming, less snow falls in the Rockies today. The river's water supply is shrinking. And along its 2,200-mile journey from Colorado to the Gulf of California, the river grows saltier and saltier. It picks up minerals from desert soils and agricultural runoff. Dams that hold back the river's natural flow have made the problem worse by preventing seasonal rainstorms from flushing salts and pollution from the river basin.

CAP aqueduct snaking across southern Arizona's desert west of Phoenix —Photo courtesy of the Central Arizona Project

COLORADO RIVER MAP

WYOMING

NEVADA

UTAH

COLORADO

Las Vegas

Glen Canyon Dam

Lake Powell

Lake Mead

Hoover Dam

CALIFORNIA

Lake Havasu

Parker Dam

ARIZONA

NEW MEXICO

PACIFIC OCEAN

dams

Phoenix

Yuma

CENTRAL ARIZONA PROJECT

Tucson

GULF OF CALIFORNIA

MEXICO

Colorado River system, dams, and the CAP
—Map courtesy of the Central Arizona Project

Seven western states—California, Arizona, Nevada, Utah, Colorado, New Mexico, and Wyoming—are sucking the Colorado River and its tributaries dry. River water supports at least 30 million people in these states and keeps western farmlands green. Only a salty trickle of water now passes through the Sonoran Desert of northwestern Mexico where the river enters the Gulf of California. This scarcity of water and its poor quality have destroyed one of the largest desert wetlands in the world—the Colorado River Delta. The river's flow has fallen by 96 percent of what early explorers saw between 1910 and 1920. What was once a great marshy wetland—the Colorado River delta—had beavers, jaguars, and abundant water birds. Productive fish spawning areas and nurseries in the delta have vanished. But there is a glimmer of hope on the horizon. New water-sharing agreements between the United States and Mexico, updated in 2012, will send more water to the riverbed. Wildlife should benefit, and such efforts might aid Mexico's fishing industry. Isolated wetlands fed by agricultural wastewater are also helping to bring wildlife back to the delta.

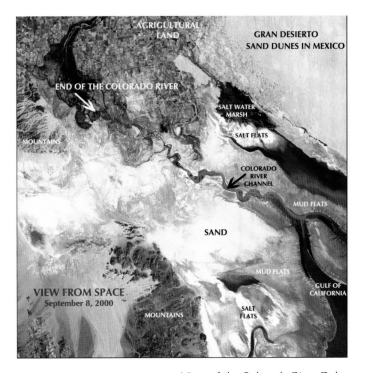

View of the Colorado River Delta from space —Photo courtesy of NASA's Earth Observatory

A 1958 photo of Mexican children carrying their catch of two giant totoaba fish. The totoaba is now a Critically Endangered species.
—Photo © Bill Beebe

Developers and resort owners show sunny pictures of palm trees, golf courses, fountains, and artificial lakes to attract homebuyers and tourists to the desert Southwest. Water prices in the desert cities of Phoenix, Las Vegas, and Palm Springs are also among the lowest in our nation. As of 2014, residents of Palm Springs and some affluent suburbs of the Greater Phoenix Metro Area were using more than 600 gallons of water per person per day! Water-loving plants and swimming pools consumed up to 70 percent of this water. The City of Phoenix averaged 108 gallons per person per day and the cities of Tucson and Los Angeles 85 to 87 gallons per day, close to the national average of 80 to 100 gallons per person per day—still about twice the amount used by most Europeans.

Water conservation in states sharing the Colorado River has for the most part been voluntary, although regulations have become necessary in Southern California because of water shortages. Los Angeles water managers tried a voluntary water conservation program, but few people changed their wasteful ways. So "water police" now patrol neighborhoods. If desert dwellers continue to view water as a resource coming from a bucket with no bottom, water conservation laws must tighten. No whining, please, when Drought Busters come knocking on your door.

Question: Florida or Arizona?

Answer: Ocotillo, a 1,900-acre development in Chandler, Arizona, with 167 acres of man-made lakes, 14 pumping stations to circulate and distribute this "reclaimed" water, and more than 33 miles of lakefront shoreline (as of 2008)

With rising water shortages, all seven states using Colorado River water are jostling for a bigger share of pie. The Colorado River Compact of 1922 established state water rights. Since then, new agreements have been drafted and amendments added to the compact, which include concerns from Mexico and Native Americans. Most of California's share irrigates fields in the Imperial Valley. Produce grown there is in high demand all over the United States. The Colorado River is already over-allocated to users. Think of it as selling too many tickets for the number of seats at a ball game. Scientists predict that by 2050, the Colorado River will be unable to provide enough water to match present expectations.

Treaties between states guarantee Arizona a set number of gallons of Colorado River water from the CAP every year. Rather than miss part of what they are entitled to, cities like Phoenix and Tucson are "banking water"—filling ponds along the CAP canal with the "extra" water. River water added to these recharge ponds sinks into the ground and mixes with native groundwater. This helps to replace water that has been pumped out over the years, a way to store water for future use. If Arizona ends up with a surplus of stored water in the years ahead, some of the state's Colorado River water "credits" can then be sold to other states to help meet their needs.

Field of lettuce in California's Imperial Valley —Bill Gates photo

Groundwater recharge ponds alongside the CAP canal about 40 miles west of Phoenix
—Photo courtesy of the Central Arizona Project

So how can we make the American Southwest a better place to live, for both people and wildlife? Desert living requires desert thinking. To fit in here, we need to respect the limitations that define this natural environment. State and city governments are beginning to think more carefully about what the region can sustain. The Arizona Department of Water Resources has produced a comprehensive statewide Water Atlas to guide water use planning. The department's educational program Project Wet introduces young people to ideas about sustainable use of water. Tucson keeps raising the price of water and has begun to turn away industries that would consume lots of water. Water managers in Los Angeles, Palm Springs, Las Vegas, and some suburbs of Phoenix are paying residents to replace lawns with drought-tolerant plants. Under this program, water savings have been big. Also, not having a swimming pool is smart desert thinking. Water evaporates quickly from pools, and few people use them regularly.

Families can easily cut indoor water use too. Installing newer toilets, low-flow showerheads, and aerators on sink faucets can save more water than you might imagine. If you just turn off the water while brushing your teeth, you can save 2 gallons of water per minute! Older toilets need about 5.5 gallons of water to flush; newer low-flow designs use as little as 0.5 gallon per flush. A low-flow showerhead can save 500 gallons of water every month. Taking shorter and fewer showers helps too. A five-minute shower uses about 20 gallons of water. Bathtubs, on the other hand, hold about 70 gallons, far more than most people need for a good bath. And keep your eyes open for leaking faucets and running toilets. A leak of only one drop per second wastes about 2,500 gallons per year.

Landscaping with plants for arid lands—with succulents, mesquite, and palo verde trees

Coal-burning Navajo Generating Station in northern Arizona, which helps to energize Phoenix, Tucson, Los Angeles, and Las Vegas

Did you know that saving water saves energy, and saving energy saves water? Water and energy are close buddies. Well pumps use energy. Purifying water takes energy. Delivering water through pipes to your home takes energy. Water heaters that give us a comfy shower use energy. Pumps that move wastewater to sewage treatment plants need energy . . . and so on. About one-fifth of California's energy budget goes into moving and treating water. In Arizona, fifteen pumping stations keep CAP water flowing uphill between the Colorado River and Tucson. Even recycling city wastewater that has been suitably cleaned ("reclaimed") for irrigation or industrial cooling requires massive amounts of energy. Transporting and cleaning water is usually the most energy-expensive public service provided by cities in the United States.

But how does saving energy save water? Most power plants use a fuel such as coal, nuclear energy, oil, or natural gas.

Burning fuel heats a fluid such as water to high temperatures, making steam. Forceful jets of steam spin blades in a turbine, which generates electricity—plus unwanted heat. Power plants must use a lot of water for cooling. In fact, in the year 2010, 38 percent of all freshwater used in the United States was helping to generate power (not including the power made at dams on rivers). In 2014, 85 percent of the electricity in the United States came from power plants fueled by nuclear energy, coal, or natural gas—coal contributed 39 percent. Nuclear plants are the most water-wasteful, and coal is next in line. You might be surprised to learn that keeping just two 60-watt light bulbs lit for seventeen hours in the West requires a gallon of cooling water at a power plant fueled by coal.

Wind machines near Palm Springs, California

On the green energy frontier, we can use sunlight and the natural forces of moving wind and water to generate electricity. Wind machines need no water to keep cool as they produce power. Energy captured from river water when it flows through turbines in a dam is another clean way to make electricity. But as global warming cuts rainfall and snowfall needed to keep rivers running, power stations at dams could run into trouble. Dams also destroy wildlife communities by greatly reducing the natural flow of rivers. Along the California coast, surfers aren't the only ones watching waves and tracking tides. Scientists are now working on ways to harness energy from the ocean's powerhouse of moving water. Heat and steam rising from deep within the earth can also be tapped as a source of energy (geothermal energy).

Sunshine is no stranger in the desert Southwest, so solar energy is getting lots of attention here. For home and business, solar cells, panels, and films allow us to tap the sun's energy directly. These devices need no cooling water. Putting a solar-powered water heater in your home is one of the best ways to trim your power use. Most large-scale solar power plants, on the other hand, concentrate the sun's energy to heat liquids to steam. So like traditional power plants, they need cooling water. But a newer design, called high gain solar, focuses sunlight on high-efficiency solar cells, a system cooled by air instead of water. Solar technology is changing faster than the desert after a summer rain, so stand by for pleasant surprises ahead.

A roof of solar panels generating electricity while shading cars in a new parking garage on the University of Arizona campus, Tucson

Rising water and energy costs will force the decline of traditional agriculture in the desert Southwest. "New" drought-tolerant crops will spread in popularity, primarily for industrial use. Dryland plants are packed with chemicals that protect them from intense sun and dry air. Many of these compounds are proving useful in industry and medicine. Plant scientists are focusing on crops that can be sold at high prices, even when the harvest is small. Allergen-free natural rubber (latex), for example, can be extracted from guayule (wy-oo-lee) shrubs, and the demand for it is increasing. Bladderpod, jojoba (ho-ho-buh), and other plants produce valuable oils, waxes, and resins that can be used in cosmetics and plastics, as well as in medicine. Wonder drugs often come from unexpected places. A new medicine for treating diabetes (Byetta), for example, came from an unusual protein discovered in Gila monster venom!

Some crops under study actually prefer salty soils. In the wild, these plants grow in coastal wetlands where desert meets the sea. Palmer saltgrass, also known as nipa (nee-pah), offers great promise as a food crop. It is drought-resistant and produces a nutritious grain similar to wheat. Biologists breeding nipa have said that this grass could become the Sonoran Desert's greatest gift to the world. Pickleweed, another native to the Sonoran Desert coast, has seeds rich in oil. New breeds of this plant offer a promising supply of vegetable oil for making organic diesel fuel (a biofuel).

Pickleweed

Sampling saliva from a Gila monster for medical research

Jojoba nuts

Tomatoes growing in southern Arizona's Nature Sweet greenhouse

Microalgae research at Arizona State University, Tempe

Some oily microscopic algae (microalgae) are mighty giants on the biofuel frontier. These simple organisms are among the oldest forms of life on Earth. Like traditional crops, green algae use sunlight, carbon dioxide, and water for growth and reproduction. But unlike traditional crops, microalgae don't need fertile farmland. They can be grown in water anywhere, even on rooftops. Microalgae could be put to work to gobble up carbon dioxide waste from power generating stations, waste that now pollutes our air. As a bonus, algae can make more oil and make it faster than other oilseed crops like soybeans and sunflowers. How? Every cell in this slimy stuff is a tiny oil factory that can process nutrients ten to twenty times faster than rooted plants can. In warm weather, microalgae grow explosively fast, especially in the sunny Southwest. Almost overnight, a neglected outdoor swimming pool will turn a yucky green. This is called an "algal bloom." Algae grow even faster in fertilized water, so they could be grown in wastewater from dairy farms, fish farms, or hydroponic greenhouses.

In hydroponic farming, plants are grown in water instead of soil, a technique that dates back some 2,000 years. Precisely controlled nutrients added to the water nourish crops. In Tucson, hydroponically grown lettuce needs only about 10 percent of the water required by field-grown lettuce. This Bibb lettuce matures from seed to a full head in just thirty-six days, and it's pesticide-free. Premium quality tomatoes and cucumbers are also grown in southern Arizona, within glass greenhouses covering more than 300 acres. Success requires good water quality, careful engineering, plant specialists, and a site that's not too hot or too cool for the crop.

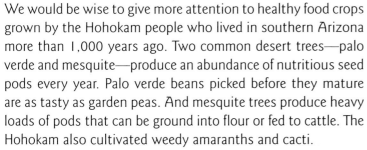

"Nopalitos" and "cactus pears" from a Tucson grocery store

Mesquite branch with seed pods

We would be wise to give more attention to healthy food crops grown by the Hohokam people who lived in southern Arizona more than 1,000 years ago. Two common desert trees—palo verde and mesquite—produce an abundance of nutritious seed pods every year. Palo verde beans picked before they mature are as tasty as garden peas. And mesquite trees produce heavy loads of pods that can be ground into flour or fed to cattle. The Hohokam also cultivated weedy amaranths and cacti.

Cacti, agaves, and other succulents are well adapted to dry climates and could be grown as crops. Mexicans make cord from hesperaloe, a relative of the century plant. Its long, strong fibers are perfect for making paper. Growing cactus is a thriving industry in rural Mexico. Prickly pear cactus fruit ("tunas" or "cactus pears") and the plants' succulent stems provide foods for both people and livestock. Spineless and seedless varieties are available too. The fruit is delicious, and the plants' young, edible pads ("nopalitos" or "cactus tenders") can be stir-fried, roasted, or pickled. Few farmers in the United States cultivate prickly pear cactus. Yet cactus tenders are growing in popularity, especially among Mexican Americans. Some farm economists predict that cactus will become a new cash crop in the Southwest.

Planting thickets of native prickly pear cacti on "retired" farmland is a quick and inexpensive way to control erosion and restore wildlife habitat. Chop off a few cactus pads, bury the cut ends in soil, and new plants will grow—no watering or follow-up care needed. In the Sonoran Desert, these cacti provide many birds, mammals, reptiles, and insects with both food and shelter. Javelina and quail, hunters' favorites, thrive in such habitats.

In 2008, Arizona began to reward people for harvesting rainwater. Taxes are lower on new homes that capture rainwater. With Tucson's average rainfall of about 12 inches per year, runoff from a 5,000-square-foot surface—such as a roof or solar panels—can yield 37,400 gallons of stored water in a year. That's 102 gallons for use every day. For the past three years, a family of two living in Tucson's desert foothills has met all of their water needs by harvesting rooftop rainwater. The runoff flows into a 26,000-gallon underground storage tank. Even with a small swimming pool and a small garden, they are enjoying a surplus of water. This shows what people can do with careful planning.

Adding a water harvesting system is just one of many ways to improve a house for desert living. The sun follows a different path as seasons change, and architects can design new homes with this in mind. If properly placed, big windows will get little direct sun in the summer but receive full sun in the winter. Covered porches and courtyards of the right size and shape can provide enjoyable outdoor living space year-around. Outside walls painted a light color reflect heat better than dark ones. High ceilings and thick insulation help to keep a house comfortable in all seasons. You can light up dark rooms and closets in the day with skylights. Consider adding solar panels and appliances that save water and energy. And remember the value of landscaping with desert plants. Look for government-sponsored discounts and tax breaks for making such improvements. When real estate developers build "Anywhere, USA" style housing that's poorly suited to the Southwest, buyers can press for better design. Smart shoppers keep informed. Are you a smart shopper?

SOLAR WATER HEATER

Tucson home with a rainwater harvesting system and solar water heater

People keep moving from places *with* water to places *without* water. We keep forgetting how power and water are connected. The future is much clearer than a glass of Colorado River water—trouble lies ahead. Slowing population growth is essential to conserving scarce resources in arid lands. Instead of trying to change the desert into something it isn't, we must learn to live in harmony with this environment. We should welcome new and sustainable ways of living in the Southwest. Wild plants and animals have time-tested secrets to share. *They* have learned to live within the limits of what the desert has to offer . . . and so must we.

A garden landscaped with native plants

Tucson, Arizona

GLOSSARY

adaptation. A trait or change in an organism's structure or behavior that helps it to survive in its environment.

amphibian. A group of animals with backbones (vertebrates) that have a body covered with soft, moist skin without scales, feathers, or hair. Most spend part of their lives in water and part on land. Typically, they lay eggs in water, developing into fishlike larvae. At metamorphosis, their larvae grow legs and lungs for life on land. This group includes frogs, toads, salamanders, newts, and wormlike caecilians.

antler. One of two bony growths, usually branched, on the head of a mammal in the deer family. Antlers fall off after the mating season and grow back the following year.

arroyo. Also known as a "wash." A stream or river channel that is usually dry and only fills after heavy rainstorms.

arthropods. A major group of invertebrate animals (those without backbones) that possess an armorlike external skeleton, segmented bodies, and jointed legs. Insects, spiders, mites, ticks, millipedes, centipedes, scorpions, and crabs are common members of the Arthropoda.

biofuel. A fuel usually derived from living or recently dead plant matter.

bird. A group of animals with backbones (vertebrates) that have a body covered with feathers, skin, and scales. All lay eggs in shells. All have wings and most can fly.

broadleaf tree. Any tree with broad, flat leaves, in contrast to trees with needlelike or scalelike leaves (such as pine trees and juniper trees).

buck. The adult male of some animals, such as deer, antelope, and rabbits.

burrow. Any hole an animal makes for shelter, usually in the ground.

camouflage. (CAM-uh-flazh). Protective colors or patterns that help an animal to blend in with its environment to escape the eyes of predators.

cholla. The common name for a group of related species of shrubby cactus plants with jointed, rounded stems. A thin, paperlike sheath covers their spines. Chollas are close relatives of prickly pear cactuses, which have flattened stems called pads.

conenose bug. A group of blood-sucking insects with soft, flattened bodies and cone-shaped heads. They are also called "kissing bugs" because they sometimes bite people near the mouth.

delta. A triangular deposit of sand and soil at the mouth of a river where it flows into another body of water (the ocean, for example).

doe. "A deer, a female deer."

drought. An extended period of water shortage.

energy. A property of matter that makes things move or change, including the flow of heat or electricity.

ewe. A female sheep.

exotic. A plant or animal transported by people to a place where it does not naturally occur.

fertilize. The union of male reproductive cells (sperm) with female egg cells, triggering rapid cell division and the growth of a baby animal or, in the case of flowering plants, the development of a seed.

flash flood. In places that are normally dry, a localized and short-lived rush of rainwater that flows into streambeds faster than it can soak into the ground. Flash floods can be unexpected and dangerous because they may hit a sunny dry area downslope from a severe storm miles away.

freshwater. Water with a very low concentration of dissolved salts.

frostbite. Damage to plant or animal tissues from exposure to freezing temperatures.

global warming. Gradual increase in Earth's surface temperature. As carbon dioxide emissions have climbed in our atmosphere over the last one hundred years, temperatures have risen dramatically worldwide. Carbon dioxide traps the sun's heat.

green energy. Sources of energy that are considered to be environmentally friendly and nonpolluting, such as moving wind or water and solar power.

groundwater. Water normally found underground and obtained from wells. In contrast, surface water can be seen in streams, rivers, ponds, and lakes.

insect. An invertebrate animal, an arthropod, with three distinct body parts, six legs, and typically one or two pair of wings.

leaf-fall. In places where climate varies from season to season, leafy plants often drop their leaves to protect themselves from moisture loss or freezing temperatures. To trigger this, plants seal off veins carrying fluids to and from their leaves.

mammal. A group of animals with backbones (vertebrates) that nourish their young with milk, have hair, and have a well-developed brain. Some, such as Australia's duck-billed platypus, lay eggs, but most give birth to live young. People are mammals, as are elephants, dogs, horses, mice, kangaroos, and many other familiar furry animals.

millipede and centipede. Invertebrate animals, arthropods, having an external skeleton divided into many similar segments, most with jointed legs. Millipedes have two pairs of legs per body segment, and centipedes have one pair per segment. Centipedes are active hunters, while most millipedes eat plant matter.

mineral salts. As used in this book, a wide array of chemicals such as calcium, sodium, chloride, sodium chloride (table salt), sulfate, magnesium, iron, carbonate, and borax that enter water with the natural weathering of rocks and soil. Salts are present in freshwater, groundwater, and seawater, in varying amounts. In high concentrations, salts can be toxic to living organisms.

monsoon. A seasonal shift in wind direction that brings moist air and heavy rainfall.

native. An organism that has existed naturally in an area without ever having been transported there by people.

nectar. A sweet liquid produced by plants, most often by their flowers, to attract animals for pollination or protection. Aggressive ants may feed on nectar and in turn protect the plant from plant-eating animals.

nocturnal. Active at night.

off-road vehicle (ORV). Any motorized vehicle capable of cross-country travel on land, water, snow, or other natural terrain.

paralyze. To make an animal unable to move or act.

photosynthesis. The chemical process utilized by green plants and some microorganisms to capture the energy from visible light and convert it into stored food energy. This process consumes water and carbon dioxide and releases oxygen gas as a waste product that is essential for the survival of most animals, including us.

pollen. Tiny capsules (grains) produced by flowering plants that contain male reproductive cells (sperm). For seeds to be made, pollen must be transferred to a flower's female reproductive organ (the pistil), so fertilization can occur. This may be done by wind or by animals (pollinators) such as insects or birds.

power plant. A complex of structures, machinery, and equipment for generating electrical energy from another source of energy such as coal, the sun, or moving water.

predator. Any animal that hunts and eats another animal.

prey. The animal that a predator eats.

pupil. The opening in the front of the eye that allows light to enter the lens, which in turn focuses light and images on the sensitive inner lining (retina) of the eyeball. The size and shape of the pupil is controlled by the surrounding circular band of muscle (iris), the colored part of the eye.

rainwater harvesting. Collecting, storing, and redirecting rainwater for beneficial use.

ram. A male sheep.

reclaimed water. Domestic wastewater treated enough to allow its reuse for landscape and agricultural irrigation, industrial cooling, and groundwater recharging. Further treatment through desalination and water purification technologies can make reclaimed water safe for drinking.

reptile. A large group of animals with backbones (vertebrates) that have a body covered with protective scales. This group includes dinosaurs of ages past, alligators and crocodiles, turtles and tortoises, lizards and snakes, and a primitive lizardlike creature native to New Zealand called the "tuatara." Because birds evolved from a line of dinosaurs, many modern biologists consider birds reptiles too!

salinity. The total amount of dissolved solids (TDS) in a water sample.

scorpion. Ancient invertebrate animals, arthropods, closely related to spiders. Like spiders, they have eight legs and two main body parts. But unlike spiders they have a tail with six segments ending in a stinger with venom glands. And unlike most spiders, scorpions cannot spin silk and they give birth to live young.

semiarid. Land that often borders deserts, receives 10 to 20 inches of annual rainfall, and often supports scrubby vegetation and short, coarse grasses.

soil crust. Soil crusts come in two types: (1) physical soil crust, which is an inorganic hardening of the soil surface—examples include a crust of mineral salts and crusts formed by trampling; and (2) biological soil crust, which is formed by living organisms that bind surface soil particles together with organic substances.

spawning. A method of sexual reproduction in which females release their eggs in water where they mix with and are fertilized by sperm added by males. Many animals that spend all or most of their lives in the water—such as fish, corals, and some amphibians—breed in this manner.

species. A population or populations of genetically similar plants or animals that under natural conditions can only breed with others of their own kind. In every scientific name, such as *Lepus alleni*, the first word is the genus (a group of closely related species—*Lepus* represents six species of jackrabbits). And the second part of the name is the species, in this case one kind of jackrabbit, the antelope jackrabbit.

spider. Invertebrate animals, arthropods, with two main body parts, eight legs, and fangs that inject venom. Modified limbs on the abdomen spin silk. Unlike most other arthropods, spiders have no antennae. Mites, ticks, and scorpions are closely related to spiders—all are arachnids.

spine. Any strong, sharp-tipped spike on a plant or animal's surface, often providing protection from predators. The word is also used to describe the row of bones that surround and protect the spinal cord.

succulent. Any plant that conserves water by storing it in fleshy leaves or stems.

sustainable living. To live in a manner that preserves our environment and protects it for the well-being of generations to come.

tadpole. Sometimes called a pollywog. A fishlike stage in the development of a frog, toad, or salamander.

venomous. Animals that typically inject a toxic substance into their prey when hunting or, as a means of defense, into would-be predators.

wetland. A wildlife habitat with soil that is regularly wet or flooded. Swamps, marshes, estuaries, and bogs are typical wetlands. They can be freshwater or saltwater habitats.

RECOMMENDED RESOURCES FOR STUDENTS AND TEACHERS

WEBSITES

Arizona-Sonora Desert Museum   www.desertmuseum.org
Without question, this is the most comprehensive website about the Sonoran Desert on the Internet. It's filled with Fact Sheets, an Especially for Kids section, Desert Questions & Answers, practical advice for desert living, bilingual resources for Hispanic children, community outreach programs, and Teacher Resources for different grade levels.

Biological Soil Crusts   www.soilcrust.org/
A fascinating website compiled by the Canyonlands Research Station of the U.S. Geological Survey. Click on "CRUST 101" for a simplified introduction to biological soil crusts or download an advanced PDF file for a deeper understanding.

Invasive Plants
www.nps.gov/sagu/naturescience/invasive-plants.htm
www.hcn.org/issues/352/17167
Provides an overview of introduced grasses and other weedy plants that pose serious threats to desert ecosystems.

The Desert Environment
http://education.nationalgeographic.com/education/encyclopedia/desert/?ar_a=1

http://en.wikipedia.org/wiki/Desert

http://en.wikipedia.org/wiki/List_of_deserts

http://www.eoearth.org/topics/view/51cbfc80f702fc2ba812b489/ :: Encyclopedia of Earth – Deserts of the World

DesertUSA   www.desertusa.com
This is one of the largest and most useful commercial websites about desert regions of the American West. It's managed by a San Diego–based multimedia company. Their stated goal is to entertain, educate, and explore the beauty, life, and culture of the North American deserts. Along with lots of advertising, you'll find archives of fascinating articles, travel and photography tips, recipes, real-time wildflower updates, maps, and a wealth of educational resources, including a kid-friendly glossary.

Green Facts   www.greenfacts.org
A website packed with clear, concise summaries of scientific reports on environmental and health topics ranging from energy and genetically modified crops to climate change and the spread of man-made deserts (desertification). A website well worth exploring.

Law of the River :: website of the Colorado River Water Users Association
www.crwua.org/colorado-river/uses/law-of-the-river
Seven states depend on dwindling water supplies of the Colorado River. In this website you'll find a wealth of information about its history, treaties, maps, dams, and current resolutions. Be sure to check out this timeline from 1869-present: www.crwua.org/documents/about-us/Timeline_final.pdf

National Park Service   www.nps.gov
Spectacular desert habitats and ancient ruins in the American West have been preserved for all to enjoy, and this website is rich in resources about them all. Some educational programs are especially well developed. Saguaro National Park, for example, offers opportunities for school field trips and park ranger visits to the classroom free of charge, complete with curriculum materials for teachers. Use this link to search for topics of interest by name or location on a map of the United States: www.nps.gov/findapark/index.htm.

Running Dry   www.runningdry.org
A timely website that features news briefs, articles, videos, and books that focus on the water crisis worldwide. Its organizers—a nonprofit corporation called The Chronicles Group, Inc.—aim to raise public awareness about water conservation, sustainability, and safety.

Union of Concerned Scientists www.ucsusa.org

Political and economic interests often distort scientific information delivered to the public. This watchdog group of concerned scientists and citizens aims to counter this trend by offering credible research to help others make informed decisions. Topics given special attention include global warming, energy, vehicles, threats to international security, invasive species, and sustainable agriculture.

U. S. Department of Energy

www.energy.gov/science-innovation/scienc-educcation

A website filled with energy trends, facts, definitions, statistics, and suggestions for saving energy at home. The material is well organized and clearly written. Here you can also find information on contests, scholarships, and energy-related career opportunities (listed under Human Resources).

Water Webster http://waterwebster.org

This useful website is a well-organized portal with hundreds of links to other water-related websites, covering everything from agencies and foundations to desalination, maps, and water quality testing. Coverage is both national and international. For news about the Colorado River, go to waterwebster.org/ColoradoRiver.htm.

BOOKS FOR TEENAGERS AND ADULTS

Arritt, Susan. 1993. *The Living Earth Book of Deserts*. Pleasantville, NY: Reader's Digest.

A beautiful big-budget book that takes readers on a guided tour through the world's deserts. An enjoyable blend of history, scientific phenomena, geological wonders, and desert ecology, with people included throughout. Forty-six pages of unique backmatter profile thirty-one distinctive deserts of the world. Packed with stunning photos and informative illustrations. One of my favorites!

Braus, Judy, Ed. 1998. *Discovering Deserts* (Ranger Rick's Nature-Scope Series). Reston, VA: The National Wildlife Federation.

This two-color teacher's guide contains background information and activities designed to help children learn about desert climates, plants, animals, and people. Material can be adapted by teachers for students at any elementary level. Includes activity pages for copying.

Brewer, Linda M. 2011. *Vanishing Circles: Portraits of Disappearing Wildlife of the Sonoran Desert Region*. Tucson, AZ: Arizona-Sonora Desert Museum.

The text of this lavish book celebrates 67 rare and endangered species and seven ecological regions, while showcasing the work of 27 talented artists in color throughout. Includes conservation information, a map, reading resources, species list, glossary, and an index.

Evans, Doris. 2001. *Let's Explore the Desert, a Family Go Guide*. Tucson, AZ: Arizona-Sonora Desert Museum.

A fun, well-written guide to help parents introduce children to the wonders of the Sonoran Desert, presented in a question-answer format. Learning resources, family hikes, and other activities can be found in the backmatter. "Cool Facts" throughout, with a few black-and-white photos.

Hayes, Allan (Author), Carl Hayes (Author), Anne Woosley (Foreword), and John Blom (Photographer). 2006. *The Desert Southwest: Four Thousand Years of Life and Art*. Berkeley, CA: Ten Speed Press.

A beautiful and scholarly reference book about the human history in desert lands stretching across southern California, southern Arizona, southern New Mexico, and northern Mexico. Emphasis on accomplishments, conflicts, and arts/crafts, especially pottery. Richly illustrated with maps and photographs. Excellent bibliography and index.

Lancaster, Brad. 2006 (vol. 1); 2008 (vol. 2). *Rainwater Harvesting for Drylands and Beyond*. Tucson, AZ: Rainsource Press. [See www.HarvestingRainwater.com.]

This award-winning two-volume set (with a third volume in the works) provides extensive background on the nature of rain and how people use water. But most importantly, these are hands-on guidebooks for designing, implementing, and maintaining home water-harvesting systems for landscaping in arid climates. The books also contain helpful glossaries and useful resources.

Lazaroff, David W. 1998. *Arizona-Sonora Desert Museum Book of Answers*. Tucson, AZ: Arizona-Sonora Desert Museum.

Visitors to the Arizona-Sonora Desert Museum have many questions about the Sonoran Desert, and this book features some of those most commonly asked. Staff scientists give detailed answers to forty-two of these questions. The book includes valuable resources in the back, such as first aid for venomous bites, a glossary, additional reading, and a list of desert parks with contact information.

Merlin, Pinau (Author), and Pamela Ensign (Illustrator). 2003. *A Field Guide to Desert Holes*. Tucson, AZ: Arizona-Sonora Desert Museum.

A guide to help desert explorers of any age to sort through the multitude of holes, depressions, mounds, and shelters of desert critters. This book is packed with useful natural history notes about desert wildlife. But accurately identifying "who lives here" is challenging, so each description carries a "Possible Builder/Occupant" notation.

Olin, George. 1994. *House in the Sun: A Natural History of the Sonoran Desert*. Tucson, AZ: Western National Parks Association.

A chatty overview of climate, geology, and the rich diversity of plant and animal life in the Sonoran Desert. Includes mountain islands within this sea of desert lowlands as well as perspectives on human survival in arid lands. Material is presented in a friendly, nontechnical style. Informative illustrations and photos.

Philips, Steven J., and Patricia W. Comus, Eds. 2000. *A Natural History of the Sonoran Desert*. Tucson, AZ: Arizona-Sonora Desert Museum Press; Berkeley, CA: University of California Press.

This user-friendly black-and-white compendium of information about the Sonoran Desert has become *the* most important and authoritative general reference book on the subject. Teachers and writers presenting material on deserts should have this book in hand. Its introductory overview sections are especially valuable. And 456 pages of its 628 pages are devoted to brief plant/animal profiles.

CHILDREN'S NONFICTION

Baylor, Byrd (Author), and Peter Parnall (Illustrator). 1987. *The Desert Is Theirs*. New York, NY: Aladdin Books.

Grades 3-5

All elementary school libraries should own this Caldecott Honored Book. In every respect it's a masterful work . . . simple, poetic, meaningful, and exquisitely illustrated. And don't think for a minute that it's fiction. Although it does include a creation legend, the writing is based on real values held by today's Desert People, the Tohono O'odham (Papago), indigenous to the Sonoran Desert. The O'odham humbly respect their place in a desert world shared with other living things, a message eloquently conveyed by Byrd Baylor.

Gowan, Barbara. 2012. *D is for Desert: A World Deserts Alphabet*. Ann Arbor, MI: Sleeping Bear Press.

Ages 6-9, Grades 2-5

Letters of the alphabet introduce one-page themes about deserts of the world, with beautiful illustrations by Gijsbert van Frankenhuyzen. Some topics focus on physical features of the land and its people, others on plants and animals. Each page has four lines of text (sometimes rhyming) for young readers and sidebars with about 25 lines of informative text for more advanced readers. The text jumps all over the world, yet there's no map to show children where these places are. Includes a glossary but no index.

MacQuitty, Miranda. 2000. *Desert* (Eyewitness Books Series). New York, NY: Dorling Kindersley.

Grades 6-10

A characteristically rich DK potpourri of photo cut-outs with fascinating bits of information (in very tiny type) across a wide range of topics. Factoids about all deserts of the world are mixed in page spreads covering the basics of what deserts are to specifics about geology, plant/animal adaptations, domesticated animals, human dwellings, food, clothing, and arts. Conservation concerns are next-to-none in this "gee-whiz" book.

Sayre, April Pulley. 1994. *Desert* (Exploring Earth's Biomes Series). New York, NY: 21st Century Books/Henry Holt & Co.

Ages 9-12, Grades 4-8

Although visually uninspiring because of its crude maps, few photos, and old-textbook design style, information in these pages is well organized and more accurate than most other children's books on the subject. One chapter is devoted to North American deserts, but most of the book focuses on principles that apply to deserts worldwide, appropriate for a biomes series.

Wallace, Marianne D. 2009. *America's Deserts: A Guide to Plants and Animals*. Golden, CO: Fulcrum Publishing.

Grades 3-5

North American's four desert regions compared, with each discussed separately and highlighted on a large regional base map repeated six times in the book. Pages are packed with tiny illustrations of common plants and animals—120 of them—half of them in color.

Warhol, Tom. 2007. *Deserts (Earth's Biomes Series)*. Tarrytown, NY: Marshall Cavendish Benchmark.

Grades 6-10

More of a short reference book, with interesting text that focuses on desert geology, plant and animal adaptations, and different types of deserts around the world (half of the book) . . . yet polar deserts aren't discussed. The two maps and author's definition of *desert* are surprisingly inaccurate. Illustrations are limited to small world maps that highlight hot and temperate desert areas, with supporting photos throughout.

Warren, Scott. 1997. *Desert Dwellers: Native Peoples of the American Southwest*. San Francisco, CA: Chronicle Books.

Ages 9-12

Introductory profiles of native peoples in the American Southwest—Pueblo and Pai groups, Hopi, Apache, Navajo, and Pima/Tohono O'odham. Contains little information about how people make the most of limited desert resources. Focus is on history, lifestyles, religion, arts, and ceremonies. Solid text accompanied by color photographs.

Wright-Frierson, Virginia. 1996. *A Desert Scrapbook, Dawn to Dusk in the Sonoran Desert*. New York, NY: Simon and Schuster Books for Young Readers.

Ages 6-10

An artist's view of the Sonoran Desert. Beautiful watercolor sketches and text show/tell what the author has found and observed in the desert around Tucson, Arizona.

SPANISH/BILINGUAL TITLES

Bash, Barbara. 1993. *El Gigante del Desierto (El Mundo del Saguaro)*. New York, NY: Scholastic.

———. 2002. *Desert Giant: The World of the Saguaro Cactus*. San Francisco, CA: Sierra Club Books for Children.

Ages 6-10

You can find several children's books about life in, on, and around the saguaro cactus, and this one is my favorite. The well-written text is tightly focused and, for the most part, biologically accurate. Engaging illustrations. No backmatter.

Evans, Doris, and Jesus Garcia. 1998. *Desert Life, A Vocabulary / Vida Desertica, Vocabulario*. Tucson, AZ: Arizona-Sonora Desert Museum.

This useful pocket-sized paperback is exactly as promoted on its back cover: " . . . a handy bilingual reference book for students, teachers, scientists, writers and anyone else who is interested in terms that describe the natural history of the Sonoran Desert region. . . ."

Jackson, Kate, and Natalie Rowe (Illustrator). *Katie of the Sonoran Desert / Katie del Desierto Sonorense*. 2009. Tucson, AZ: Arizona-Sonora Desert Museum.

Ages 6-12

This winner of two nonfiction book awards follows the life of a western diamondback rattlesnake and two reptile specialists who track them. It's a personalized story told from the snake's point of view that illustrates difficulties in surviving as a rattlesnake in the Sonoran Desert. 71 pages of bilingual text, color illustrations, descriptions of animals, a glossary, a map, but no index.

Rivera-Ashford, Roni Capin (Author), and Richard Johnsen (Illustrator). *Hip, Hip, Hooray, It's Monsoon Day! / ¡Ajúa, Ya Llegó el Chubasco!* 2007. Tucson, AZ: Arizona-Sonora Desert Museum.

Grades 2-5

An excellent bilingual reader for students. This is an engaging story about one family's experience when the summer monsoon season arrives in the desert Southwest. It includes Mexican family traditions, detailed information about this weather phenomenon, and helpful learning resources in the back. The illustrator's watercolor landscapes are strong, but his human figures aren't nearly as good.

SCIENTIFIC NAMES OF ANIMALS SHOWN IN THIS BOOK

Animals Without Backbones: Invertebrates

Insects

cactus longhorn beetle, *Moneilema gigas*

conenose bug (desert kissing bug), *Triatoma rubida*

golden paper wasp, *Polistes aurifer*

gulf fritillary, *Agraulis vanillae*

honeybee, *Apis mellifera*

horse lubber grasshopper, *Taeniopoda eques*

monarch butterfly, *Danaus plexippus*

painted lady butterfly, *Vanessa cardui*

Spiders and Scorpions

bark scorpion, *Centruoides sculpturatus*

desert blond tarantula, *Aphonopelma chalcodes*

giant red velvet mite, *Dinothrombium magnificum* or *D. superbum*

Millepedes and Centipedes

desert millipede (rainworm), *Orthoporus ornatus*

giant desert centipede, *Scolopendra heros*

Animals with Backbones: Vertebrates

Fish

totoaba, *Totoaba macdonaldi*

Amphibians and Reptiles

collared lizard, *Crotaphytus collaris*

desert iguana, *Dipsosaurus dorsalis*

desert tortoise, *Gopherus agassizii*

Gila monster, *Heloderma suspectum*

regal horned lizard, *Phrynosoma solare*

spadefoot toads: Couch's spadefoot, *Scaphiopus couchii*;
   and Mexican spadefoot, *Spea multiplicata*

western diamondback rattlesnake, *Crotalus atrox*

zebra-tailed lizard, *Callisaurus draconoides*

Birds

black-chinned hummingbird, *Archilochus alexandri*

cactus wren, *Campylorhynchus brunneicapillus*

curve-billed thrasher, *Toxostoma curvirostre*

elf owl, *Micrathene whitneyi*

Gambel's quail, *Callipepla gambelii*

Gila woodpecker, *Melanerpes uropygialis*

great horned owl, *Bubo virginianus*

Harris' hawk, *Parabuteo unicinctus*

mourning dove, *Zenaida macroura*

roadrunner, *Geococcyx californianus*

white-winged dove, *Zenaida asiatica*

Mammals

antelope jackrabbit, *Lepus alleni*

bobcat, *Lynx rufus*

cactus mouse, *Peromyscus eremicus*

collared peccary (javelina), *Pecari tajacu*

coyote, *Canis latrans*

desert bighorn sheep, *Ovis canadensis nelsoni*

grasshopper mouse, *Onychomys torridus*

Harris' antelope squirrel, *Ammospermophilus harrisii*

kit fox, *Vulpes macrotis*

lesser long-nosed bat, *Leptonycteris curasoae*

Merriam's kangaroo rat, *Dipodomys merriami*

mountain lion (cougar), *Puma concolor*

mule deer, *Odocoileus hemionus*

Native American woman (Tohono O'odham), *Homo sapiens*

rabbit (desert cottontail), *Sylvilagus audubonii*

round-tailed ground squirrel, *Spermophilus tereticaudus*

white-tailed deer, *Odocoileus virginianus couesi*

SCIENTIFIC NAMES OF PLANTS MENTIONED IN THIS BOOK

Wildflowers, Vines, Grasses

bladderpod, *Physaria gordonii*

buffelgrass, *Pennisetum ciliare*

desert lupine, *Lupinus sparsiflorus*

desert marigold, *Baileya multiradiata*

dune evening-primrose, *Oenothera deltoides*

dune sunflower (showy sunflower), *Helianthus niveus tephrodes*

goldfields, *Lasthenia gracilis*

Mexican gold poppy, *Eschscholzia californica mexicana*

owl's clover (escobita), *Castilleja exserta*

Palmer saltgrass (Palmer grass), *Distichlis palmeri*

sand verbena (dune verbena), *Abronia villosa*

tepary bean, *Phaseolus acutifolius*

Succulents

century plant (agave), *Agave deserti*

cholla cactus, *Cylindropuntia fulgida*

fishhook barrel cactus, *Ferocactus wislizeni*

hedgehog cactus, *Echinocereus fendleri*

hesperaloe, *Hesperaloe funifera*

ocotillo, *Fouquieria splendens*

organ pipe cactus, *Stenocereus thurberi*

pickleweed, *Salicornia bigelovii*

prickly pear cactus, *Opuntia engelmannii*

saguaro cactus, *Carnegiea gigantea*

staghorn cholla, *Cylindropuntia versicolor*

Trees and Shrubs

Arizona black walnut, *Juglans major*

Arizona sycamore, *Platanus wrightii*

creosotebush, *Larrea divaricata* variety *tridentata*

desert broom, *Baccharis sarothroides*

Fremont cottonwood, *Populus fremontii*

guayule, *Parthenium argentatum*

jojoba, *Simmondsia chinensis*

palo verde, *Parkinsonia (Cercidium) florida* = *Parkinsonia microphylla*

velvet ash, *Fraxinus velutina*

velvet mesquite, *Prosopis velutina*

willow, *Salix* species

INDEX

ABOUT THE AUTHOR

Thomas Wiewandt is a natural history photographer with a Ph.D. in ecology from Cornell. A native to the American Southwest, he has pursued a career that blends science, art, ecotourism, and publishing. His motion picture films for the BBC and the National Geographic Society captured an Emmy nomination in cinematography, a Gold Apple Award at the National Educational Film and Video Festival, and four Cine Golden Eagles. His self-published book *The Southwest Inside Out* (2001, 2004) was awarded four top regional and national honors.

This greatly expanded edition of *Hidden Life of the Desert* follows in the footsteps of a Crown (1990) edition that made the John Burrough's List of Outstanding Nature Books for Young Readers. It also serves as the companion book to Tom's independently produced film Desert Dreams, which can be seen on Public Television across America, starting in August 2015. For more information, visit www.wildhorizons.com.